OCCUPATIONAL ENGLISH TEST

SPEAKING FOR NURSES

By Virginia Allum

D1633581

ISBN 978-1-291-83912-8

C20404364 PE GRH

CONTENTS

OET speaking test – What is it like?

The obvious thing about the OET is that it is a medical English test for any of 12 health care professionals. The topics in the speaking test relate to your healthcare area, however, like other language tests, it is a language test.

As I said, it sounds obvious but sometimes it's easy to forget that, as it can appear to be similar to the tests that healthcare professionals do during their degrees. The reading and the listening tests are the same for all groups. This means that you will be reading a text or texts about a health topic e.g. heart disease, stem cell research, prevention of dental caries and so on. The same goes for the listening test. You may be listening to a consultation between a doctor and a patient about measles or treatment of a sport's injury.

So, to repeat the important part about the role plays. **They are a test of your ability to communicate**. They are not a test of your knowledge of the medical condition – the subject of the role play. This is the difference between the OET role plays and the sort of role plays you may have done with OSCAS or OSCES during your degree.

The OSCE tests your nursing / medical/ physiotherapy knowledge in a particular area as well as your ability to communicate with the patient. The OET concentrates on your ability to communicate during a scenario.

Obviously you need to know some relevant vocabulary but it's the way you get your message across that is more important.

What do I do with the 12.5 minutes of role play time?

The speaking test contains an initial warm-up conversation and two role plays.

The warm-up conversation:

This is a brief (2 minute) chat where the interlocutor checks and confirms your details. Remember that if you use an 'English' name but your passport uses your birth name, you may have to explain this. Be ready to explain the reason for using different names, e.g. *'My English name is Jenny. It's easier than my Korean name, Sug Ja.'*

Even though the 2 minute chat is not given a mark it is a great opportunity to relax a bit and build a rapport with the interlocutor. Try to look as though you are enjoying yourself. Smile and maintain eye contact. If you appear confident and relaxed, it makes the job of the interlocutor a lot easy.

Examples of warm-up conversations

The short warm-up conversation about you and your professional background.

This will be around 2 minutes long. You should try to have a few sentences planned for each possible question. Things which you might talk about:

1. *What do you know about life in Australia?*

Asking what you know about famous landmarks e.g. Sydney Opera House, Uluru, The Great Barrier Reef, The Barossa Valley, Kakadu National Park etc.

'What do you know about the wildlife in Australia?' Most people know about kangaroos and koalas but also platypus and wombat. What do you know about the lifestyle? – a lot of outdoor living e.g. barbecues, beach visits (most people live along the coast).

2. *What are your plans when you live in Australia?*

This question could be about whether you plan to just work or perhaps travel as well. You could talk about study plans. You may plan to stay for a few years then return home. *Are you going to live with a friend or relative already living in Australia?*

3. *Why do you want you come and work in Australia?*

This is where you explain whether you want to work in Australia to experience a different culture, to learn new skills or because you feel you will have more opportunity. You may have met an Australian boy or girl and want to come to Australia to be with them.

4. *What sort of nursing do you do at the moment?*

You will need to explain the area of nursing you are involved in and the main activities you do e.g. orthopaedic nursing in a trauma unit, medical unit specialising in burns treatment etc. You should learn the vocabulary which is appropriate to your type of nursing e.g. 'fractures' - talking about orthopaedic nursing.

What do you like about nursing children / midwifery / Intensive Care nursing? Try to think of three reasons you like the area you are working in e.g. it's fast paced, the procedures are very interesting, it's very rewarding. If you don't like the area you work in, you could explain why e.g. you don't feel that your skills are used in this area, you find the type of nursing very depressing etc.

5. *Where will you work when you move to Australia?*

Describe the area you are planning to go to even if it is still a plan e.g. *'Are you looking at one of the big cities or a small town? Are you thinking of working in a remote area?'* Prepare three or four sentences which describe the place you are considering.

The role plays

You will have to perform two role plays of around 5 minutes each. Each role play card guides you how you will conduct the role play through the list of tasks. The role play needs to follow a definite structure much in the way of the writing task. Think about how a conversation usually flows:

* You introduce yourself and explain your title.
* You find out what has happened or about what the patient knows about a problem.
* Explain something to the patient.
* Give advice about lifestyle changes, new medication, discharge activities.
* Round off your conversation

You may have to add some other strategies like persuading, empathising or reassuring. This makes the role play sound a bit more authentic.

The role play card should contain any medical knowledge that you may need. Think about ways you can explain medical terms using everyday language to your patient. To repeat – this is a language test. What the examiners are looking for is whether you can start a conversation with a patient, keep it going, manage the conversation if the patient tries to be difficult and then close the conversation.

It's a good idea to make a glossary of medical terms and their equivalent everyday terms. Start with these:

Reduce	cut down
Eliminate	cut out
Remove	take out
Sutures	Stitches

Another question that I am asked is *'What do I do if I don't know anything about the topic?'* As I said before, you will usually be given any information you need on the role play card. Sometimes you may have to make a guess. An example of this is a role play between a school nurse and a teenage boy who has scurvy. If you didn't know what scurvy is, you could guess that it has something to do with problems with the diet as later in the role play you are asked to advise the student about some diet changes he should make.

But, what if you can't guess at all what the condition or disease is? Or, you don't know what a medication does. You can do a bit of inventing. After all, we want to hear you explaining the condition or the medication. You can use expressions like these:

1. *'X is a condition that affects your skin.'*
2. *'Condition Y causes some problems with your digestion.'*
3. *'Medication B is a tablet that lowers your blood pressure.'*
4. *'You need to be careful when you take the medication. You should always take the tablets before a meal.'*

As you can see, you can always make very general statements about medical conditions. If you have to talk about a medication, you can talk about how to take it, warn about side effects and advise how long to take the medication. Remember that it doesn't have to be accurate information – it's the way you give advice that's important.

So, in summary try not to worry too much about your medical knowledge. Concentrate on communicating well. Go over the expressions you know for the most common communication examples. Practise the pronunciation of some sample dialogues.

If you can, try them out on a friend. Write your own role play and practise it. Or, use dialogues in preparation materials. There are transcripts of the dialogues I've made on the oetprep.com website. Time the role play so you have an idea of how a 5 minute role play should flow. Finally, try out some alternative phrases. Above all, focus on your ability to communicate.

Starting an OET speaking for nurses role play

After you have looked at the tasks on your role play, you should have an idea of the language the interlocutor will be expecting to hear from you. In other words, what is the purpose of the role play?

Is it :

- to give information or explain treatment
- to persuade the patient to do something or not to do something
- to empathise with the patient
- to give advice

You should be able to draw on some expressions which you have practised beforehand. But starting the role play is sometimes difficult. In authentic conversations, you will have been taught to ask open questions to encourage the patient to talk. The OET asks you to do this while doing most of the talking yourself.

There are two paths the conversation may take. The first possibility is that you will start the conversation. The second possibility is that the 'patient' will start it off. Remember that you won't have the benefit of seeing the patient's role card so it will be guess work in the beginning.

The role play cards contain around 4 tasks for you to cover. The first task is the cue for the start of the role play. The most common is a 'Find out about..' task. Some examples are:

1. Ask about... or Find out about....
1. Scurvy: Ask Jake about his class room behaviour. Ask detailed questions about his diet and lifestyle.
2. Bedwetting: Find out the out the frequency of bedwetting and if there are any other concerns.

3. Young child with epilepsy: Find out as much as you can about the boy's condition.

4. Immunisation: Find out exactly what the patient's concerns are.

5. Child with burns: Find out as much as you can about the accident and subsequent treatment of the burns.

6. Parkinson's Disease: Find out what the patient is having difficulty with.

7. Head injury: Find out as much as you can about the details of the patient's accident and any symptoms.

8. Appendectomy: Find out as much as you can about the details of the patient's accident and any symptoms.

Other 'first tasks' are:

Give the patient information about....

- Baby with jaundice: Give the patient information and advice on the condition.

- Advise on hip replacement surgery: Focus on the positive aspect of the surgery

- Mother with stroke: Explain why you are monitoring the patient.

Try to persuade....

- Resident in Nursing Home: Try to persuade the resident to take his/her medication

Discuss patient concerns

- Child with meningitis: Discuss the parents' worries

Let's look at the 'find out about...' task. Before I start, I'll go through the two conversation possibilities. I mentioned the role play that you, the nurse, starts.

If you are starting the conversation, it's important to introduce yourself and explain your position in the ward or community centre. You'll find out the information about this on the role play card. Look at the 'Setting' for some direction e.g. *'Hello, Mrs Smith. My name's Virginia. I'm a Registered Nurse on this ward.'* The setting may be a ward, the Accident and Emergency Department, a school or a workplace health centre.

If the patient starts the conversation, it may sound a little strange to introduce yourself as it may be accepted that this has already happened. As the patient starts talking, use Active Listening techniques to indicate that you are paying attention. You'll remember that this is:

- nodding your head
- saying *'Uh huh'*, *'Oh right'* and *'Mm'*
- smiling

Can you tell me about?

Then, you can look at the 'find out about' question, that is, why the patient is talking to you. In order to ask an open question, you'll use *'Can you tell me about ...?'* or *'Can you tell me how long...?'* *'Can you tell me what...?'*

Be careful with *'Can you tell me about...'* as it may be followed by a noun or a verb (with some changes). Review these forms:

'Can you tell me about .....noun / gerund?'

'Can you tell me about what/how/when/why/ where....verb....?'

'Can you tell me about <u>the pain</u>? Can you tell me <u>when you get</u>

the pain?'

*'Can you tell me about <u>your leg ulcer</u>? Can you tell me <u>where the
ulcer is?'</u>*

The verb in a *'Can you tell me where/what/who ....?'* is in reverse.
*Where **did** you **take** your son? → Can you tell me where you **took**
your son?*
*What medication **do you take**? → Can you tell me what
medication **you take**?*
*What **is** your name? → Can you tell me what your name **is?**

The difference between open and closed questions
Look at these examples from the bedwetting role play:
Closed: *'How often does he wet the bed?'* – you'd expect the
patient to say *'Every night'* or *'He wets the bed all the time'.*
Closed: *'Can you tell me how often he wets the bed?'* – similar to
the previous question
Open: *'Can you tell me about his bedwetting?'* – Notice that I had
to use a noun form (gerund)

Here are some more examples:

'What caused your daughter's injury?' - **closed**

'Can you tell me what caused your daughter's injury?' - **closed**

'Can you tell me about your daughter's injury?' – **open** question

A variation is *'Can you tell me a bit more about your daughter's injury?'*

If you want to use a verb with the 'Can you tell me about' expression, you need to add a 'wh' question word onto it, e.g.

*'Can you tell me more about **what** happened to your daughter?'*

*'Can you tell me a bit more about **how often** your son has this problem?'*

*'Can you tell me a bit more about **why** you are concerned?'*

Notice that the order of words changes in these questions:

*'How often **does** your son **have** this problem?'* becomes

*'Can you tell me a bit more about how often your son **has** this problem?'*

*'Why **are you** concerned?'* becomes .....

*'Can you tell me a bit more about why **you are** concerned?'*

Can you tell me about? The placement of prepositions

Be careful with the placement of prepositions in a question. If you are starting the conversation and are unsure of the reason for the patient's visit, you may ask:

- *Can you tell me what you are concerned about?*
- *Can you tell me what you are worried about?*
- *Can you tell me what you have difficulty with?*
- *Can you tell me what you have problems with?*

Notice that the preposition goes at the end of the question.

2. CONVERSATION STRATEGIES

Strategies to use during a role play

During the speaking test, you have to make sure that you are in control of the conversation. You are expected to start things off and to maintain the flow of the conversation. In the real world, of course, you would be trying to encourage the patient to speak as much as possible. You would make sure that your conversations were patient-centred not nurse-centred.

You would ask open questions to get the person to talk more. During the OET speaking test, you need to be doing the talking most of the time. You still need to ask open questions but you also have to ensure that you display your communication ability.

Keep in mind that the interlocutor and the assessors want to see how well you can communicate. The assessors will listen to the tape of your conversation afterwards and mark your performance. Correct grammar is quite important but sounding natural and developing a rapport with your 'patient' may be just as important.

The sort of skills you need to show are:
1. introducing yourself and opening the conversation
2. asking open questions to encourage the patient to speak
3. taking turns in the conversation
4. summarising what you have said or what the 'patient' says
5. encouraging the 'patient' to change or try something
6. closing the conversation

Plan out the timing of the conversation. You have five minutes for each role play. You could plan it out like this:

< 1 min Introduce yourself and say what your title is. Here are some examples:

1. *Hello, I'm Virginia. I'm the Registered Nurse looking after you today.'* (the role play is set in a hospital ward.)

2. *'Hello, thanks for coming in today. I'm Virginia, one of the Registered Nurses at this clinic.'*

(the role play is set at a Community Medical Centre.)

3. *'Hello, I'm Virginia, the School Nurse. Thanks for coming to see me.'* (the role play is set in a school.)

3-4 mins - Go through the tasks on your role play card. Notice that there may be two issues per role play. Both issues often relate to each other.

There are usually four tasks on each card. One may be 'Find out more about ...' – this is the beginning of the conversation where you hear what the problem is. Then, perhaps an 'Explain about x disease and its treatment' – you will talk about the kind of disease it is, how it may affect the patient and how it is treated.

What if I don't know anything about the disease on the role play card?

Remember that the role play is a language test. If you don't know what the disease is, describe any disease in general terms. E.g. *'I'll just explain a bit about the condition. It can be quite a serious condition if you don't look after yourself. You'll have some tests first to check your blood and possibly also a scan. The doctor will talk to you about that a bit later. I will explain everything about the tablets you'll be taking after you have the tests.'* – as you can see, this could be any illness!

You can explain medication in general terms as well – *'The tablets you are going to take make you feel a little sick if you take them on an empty stomach. It's a good idea to take them with a meal or a dry biscuit.'*

Practise the sort of language you would use to describe a disease or condition before you do the test. It's a good idea to learn the phrases you will use, e.g. 'take the whole course of antibiotics'.

You won't know what direction the 'patient' is going to take the conversation but you can assume that the 'patient' will try to be a bit difficult.

Some of the things a 'patient' may do:
1. The 'patient' keeps talking, may be upset about something that has happened – you need to politely 'jump in': e.g.
'Can I just interrupt you for a minute? I'd like to make sure that I understand what you are saying.'
'Can I just stop you now? I want to check that I understand correctly.'

Then, you can summarise what the 'patient' says to confirm that you understand. E.g.
'So, what you said was that you were walking on the street, then you fell over a rock and injured yourself.' Try to confirm understanding using steps.

2. The 'patient' won't say much. You are going to have to encourage him or her to open up. Ask open questions as often as you can, e.g.

'Can you tell me a bit more about what happened?'

'Can you explain again what happened?'

If the 'patient' still answers with one word or two, you can summarise what was said, e.g.

'I see. So you are saying that........'

'OK. So you told me that....'

You could also empathise with the 'patient' if this is relevant, e.g.

'I imagine that must have been very difficult for you.'

' That must have been very upsetting.'

3. The 'patient' tries to get you off track.

You may be trying to explain something when the 'patient' tries to move the conversation in another direction. You will have to politely redirect the 'patient' where you want the conversation to go. E.g.

'I can talk about that in a little while. Can we just get back to what we were talking about first.'

'Can I stop you there, please? I can see that you are upset about that. I will explain about that in a minute.'

4. The 'patient' is uncooperative – won't follow your advice.
In this case, you need to negotiate with your 'patient'. Some possible situations:

* a teenager has scurvy but doesn't like fruit and vegetables.

* an elderly gentleman refuses to have new tablets because they are the wrong colour.

* a young mother insists on taking her baby home even though the baby is jaundiced.

You can use expressions such as:

'Would you be willing to try eating more oranges.'

'Would you be willing to wait until the blood results come back?'

'Could you just wait for a few minutes while I check your results?'

1 min - Closing the conversation.

If you have time, summarise the conversation. You can say:

'OK. We've talked about x, y, z.'

'Just to go over what we talked about...'

Then, you can suggest that the 'patient' may like to read a leaflet about the problem:

'I have a leaflet here which will explain a bit more about burns/scurvy/IBS etc. There's a number on the back which you can call for more information.'

'I'll give you this leaflet to read. Call me if you have any more questions after you've read it.'

Or, you can ask if the 'patient' has any questions he or she would like to ask.

'Do you have any questions you'd like to ask?'

'Is there anything else you'd like to ask?'

Expressing an opinion or giving advice

Positive sentences	Negative sentences
It is (It's) + adjective + infinitive	**It is not (isn't)+ adjective + infinitive.**
It's wise to drink water in the evening rather than coffee.	*It's not essential to do all the exercises at once.*
It is (It's) + adjective + for pronoun + infinitive	**It is not (isn't)+ adjective + for pronoun + infinitive**
It's important for you to take it easy.	*It's not advisable for you to drive after the operation.*
It is (It's) adjective that + subjunctive	**It is not (isn't)+ adjective that + subjunctive**
It's essential that you take all the medication in the packet.	*It's not necessary that he use the crutches.*

Giving advice

It's advisable to wait for the test results.

It's wise to give the baby water while he is having phototherapy.

It's important for you to stay in hospital overnight.

It's not a good idea to go home before you speak to the doctor.

It would be a good idea for you to stay here.

It's not necessary to stay any longer.

It's essential that the baby stay in hospital during the treatment.

It's not advisable for you to take the baby home yet.

3. Communication Blocks

There are many barriers to effective listening or communication blocks. These blocks stop you getting your message across. Sometimes people are not aware that they are setting up blocks and wonder why they are not able to communicate easily with their patients.

There can be a variety of barriers to communicating effectively. These barriers fall into 4 groups:

1. Physical

2. Environmental

3. Social or cultural

4. Psychological

1. Physical barriers:

These are caused by anything which affects the body. For example,

- **Speech difficulties** like slurred speech, a stammer, aphasia or dysphasia (after stroke or a brain injury)

- **Hearing impairment** – including times when hearing aids are not used.

- **Sight impairment** – be aware that the sight impaired also pick up on non-verbal communication even though it may be in a different way.

- **Confusion** e.g. in dementia – it may make it difficult for a confused person to follow the conversation and respond appropriately.

- **Pain** – especially severe pain which makes it difficult to concentrate.

- **Fatigue or altered consciousness -** including tiredness caused by medication.

2. Environmental Barriers:

• **Space or distance between people.** Patients who are lying in bed with a nurse standing 'over' a person may not feel an equal participant in the conversation. Nurses who stand at the end of the bed when talking with a patient make the conversation seem like a quick exchange.

• **Noise** – loud noises or loud music can affect patients' ability to concentrate. If a conversation is important or sensitive, it is a good idea to minimise noise or music by going to a different location or asking for the music to be turned down.

• **Physical** – the arrangement of furniture in certain configurations can make a conversation seem formal or serious. For example, chairs in a straight line are less welcoming than chairs in a circle or semi-circle. A desk between patient and nurse also creates a barrier.

• **Environment** – this can be anything from room temperature to the number of people in the room. Rooms which are large but contain a small number of people can seem confronting and make people feel that there is too much attention on them.

3. Social and Cultural Barriers:

• **Low level of health literacy** – patients who have little knowledge of medical procedures or medical conditions may struggle to follow the conversation and may tune out.

• **Heavy accent** – An accent which is hard to follow can create barriers to understanding. Regional English accents can be difficult for non-native speakers as well as native-speakers.

• **Inappropriate use of jargon or medical terminology** – it is important to judge the ability of patients to understand medical terminology. Some terms have become common in general use e.g. hypertension whilst others are not common and therefore not easily understood e.g. tachycardia. Nurses should also be aware of the number of terms used between colleagues (jargon) which may not be understood by patients.

• **Intercultural factors** - this includes different expectations of the role of the nurse and also the effect of different types of non-verbal communication between cultures. Gender may also be an issue in cases where nurses do not care for patients of the opposite sex in a particular culture or religion.

4. Psychological Barriers include:

• **Anxiety, fear or stress** – These factors affect the ability to listen clearly or listen to more than one or two instructions.

• **Anger or aggression** - Patients or their relatives who are angry about their treatment may not be willing to listen to what a nurse is saying.

• **Conflicting verbal and non-verbal messages** – non-verbal communication such as pitch of voice or lack of eye contact which does not match the words used cause confusion for the listener.

Examples of poor communication

1. Being Defensive – this may happen when patients or their relatives complain about what they consider to be poor nursing care. The nurse may reply: *'It's not my fault. I do what I can when I have time but I'm very busy'.*

2. Changing the subject inappropriately – the nurse may feel uncomfortable about what the patient is saying and not know how to reply. E.g. *'Oh...ah..well let's get this dressing done now, shall* we?' Instead of discussing the patient's concerns about dying, the nurse changes the subject and talks about the patient's dressing.

3. Offering false reassurances - by suggesting that: *'Everything will be fine'* or *'I'm sure that the lump probably won't be cancerous',* the nurse is saying what s/he thinks the patient wants to know. It may be done to reassure the patient, however, it can affect the trust between the nurse and the patient and affect future communication.

4. Offering advice or giving an opinion – Of course there are times when you are supposed to offer advice or an opinion, however, there are other times when merely listening is appropriate. By 'jumping in' and giving advice before the patient has finished talking, the patient may feel that the nurse is not interested in the conversation.

5. Ignoring non-verbal cues – Non-verbal cues are often culture-based so may be difficult to pick up. There are differences even within English-speaking countries e.g. the UK, USA and Australia.

It's a good idea to be aware of non-verbal cues which you may be expected to use. Some of these are maintaining eye contact, nodding your head to indicate agreement and using 'listening words' like 'Mm' or 'Uh huh'.

6. Inappropriate means of communication - the selection of a medium of communication may be inappropriate for the message. All oral communication – face-to-face, by telephone, by phone or on television- may be misheard. If the speaker cannot be seen, there is no opportunity of picking up non-verbal cues. Sometimes it is important to follow up verbal communication with written communication. A common example is the need for a written consent before an operation. A verbal consent is not appropriate nor is it legal.

7. The message may be too complex.   Medical terminology can be difficult for lay people. The trend for using 'plain English' means that nurses are expected to explain procedures using the everyday language understood by patients.

Checklist for effective message sending

1.　Use clear language. Avoid jargon. Clearly state what it is you want the other person to understand.

2.　Check to ensure that your message has been received with no misunderstanding. If you have any doubts, get the receiver to repeat to you the content of your message.

3.　Repeat if necessary, without impatience if you think the receiver has not understood your message.

4.　Ensure content is appropriate to the comprehension level of the receiver. Simplify if necessary, but avoid child-like dialogues.

Poor Communication	How to avoid
1. Message is expressed badly or not explained clearly	Try to structure the message in steps. Limit the explanation to 3 pieces of information. E.g. *Firstly…Then…Finally…*
2. Monopolising the conversation / continual interrupting	Don't be afraid of short silences when the patient is trying to talk to you. If you feel that you need to interrupt, try

	to use an interruption as a means of confirming that you understand. E.g. *Can I just interrupt for a moment? I want to be sure that I understand what you are saying.*
3. Jumping to conclusions /assuming you understand what the patient means without listening	Be aware of non-verbal communication and make sure to use active listening skills. If you are unsure, clarify what you think the patient is saying. E.g. *So what you are saying is…., right?*
4. Reluctance to discuss sensitive or embarrassing issues / use of clichés or being flippant to avoid direct speech	Many nurses find it difficult to discuss certain issues with their patients. It is useful in these cases to start the conversation by being honest about your difficulties. E.g. *I know it is difficult to discuss these things but it may be helpful so we can make some arrangements to help you.'* (talking about moving to a hospice for end of life care)

	Some nurses use clichés (phrases which are overused) to avoid talking about sensitive issues. For instance, they may say *Don't worry, time heals all wounds* to a relative after the death of a patient. It is better to speak openly about the patient's death e.g. *I am very sorry about your father. I hope that you will feel less sad in a while.* Being flippant can make patients feel that they are being 'spoken down to' and are not an equal partner in the conversation. For example, *Come on now, it's not that bad. It's only a scratch!*
5. Poor anger management / inability to calm an angry patient	Anger which is not handled well can lead to aggressive behaviour which can be dangerous and difficult to manage. It is important to empathise with an angry patient before you continue the

	conversation. E.g. *I can see that you are very upset at the moment. Can you explain a bit more what the problem is?* If the patient or their relative speaks louder and louder, ask them to lower their voices before you continue. *Before we go on, could you speak a bit quieter so I can understand what you are saying.*
6. Lack of empathy or poor empathy skills	Empathy is the ability to **imagine** what the patient is feeling rather than say that you **know** how they are feeling. Avoid saying *I know how you feel. I had the same thing so I know all about it.* Empathetic responses include: *You must be feeling very worried about your daughter.* *I can understand that you must be concerned about the surgery.*

Poor Communication	How to avoid
7 Lack of feedback (verbal or non-verbal)	Feedback is important to ensure that the patient knows that the nurse understands what is being said. It may be verbal e.g. *I see. So you are saying that you have been in pain for the past day. Is that right?* Feedback may also be non-verbal. For example, nodding your head to show agreement, narrowing your eye brows to show you are unsure of what is being said.

4. Non-verbal communication

Non Verbal

Non-verbal behaviours *add meaning* to speech. This is called *meta-communication* or a 'message *about* a message'. Non-verbal communication helps to work out what a person's message is actually about. Non-verbal communication is *congruent* if it matches what is being said. For example,

No, I'm not too busy to help you. (said while smiling and looking at the patient) – congruent because the nurse means to say that s/he is happy to help and is not too busy to help.

No, I'm not too busy to help you. (said with a sigh and while looking at his/her watch) – incongruent because the non-verbal communication indicates that the nurse thinks s/he is too busy to help and is annoyed at being asked.

Kinesics

Kinesics is the study of body movement. Facial expressions, gestures and eye movements are the most common categories.

- **Facial Expressions** – movements of the face which communicate emotions.

- **Body movements and gestures** – the way you lean forward or lean back shows how much you want to be near another person.
- **Hand gestures** can communicate anxiety or impatience.

Eye contact

The amount of eye contact you feel comfortable with may relate to your cultural background where eye contact may be considered rude or inappropriate. In another culture, lack of eye contact may equally be considered inappropriate or even dishonest. Maintaining eye contact for the correct amount of time differs from staring which makes people uncomfortable.

Proxemics of use of Personal Space

The distance we stand from another person is also dictated by culture. People from some cultures feel comfortable standing quite close to another person where the same distance would be construed as causing discomfort in another culture. Generally, people from an Anglo-Saxon background like to have an arm's length between them where many Europeans are quite comfortable standing much closer to each other. This distance is sometimes called a person's 'personal space'.

Therapeutic Touch

Touching another person when speaking to them especially in situations where the other person is upset or distressed is called 'therapeutic touch'. Therapeutic touch may involve a touch on the forearm or on the shoulder.

There are times when therapeutic touch can be effective, however, it is very difficult to achieve. It is important to be aware of the feelings of the other person towards being touched by a stranger. Young nurses may find it difficult to know if an elderly patient would welcome a touch on the arm or may find it condescending.

5. Asking questions – interview skills

There are basic interviewing skills which apply to any interview situation e.g. asking a patient for information. Every interview has a particular goal which speakers aim to achieve by the time the interview finishes. A role play dialogue is an example of an interview. During the interview or role play, you need to listen to the patient, send and receive verbal and non-verbal messages and respond to them. Interviews may be directive or non-directive.

Directive interviews

These interviews use *closed questions* to obtain short, quick answers. Closed questions usually deal with facts. Examples of closed questions in directive interviews are *What is your sate of birth? What is your phone number?*

The person asking the questions **directs** the interview.

Non-Directive Interviews

Non-directive interviews aim to create a conversation where the patient can express their feelings or concerns. The nurse may still guide the interview but will try not to dominate or direct it completely. They use *open questions* to explore more details about what has happened, what the concern is or what the patient knows about a procedure. Examples of open questions are *Can you tell me a bit more what happened yesterday? Can you give me some more information about the pain you've been having?*

Preparing for the interview /role play

Before you start the role play, prepare everything you want to say. Make a plan using the background information on the role play cards. Think about the type of interview or role play. You need to plan the conversation following a structure which includes a beginning and ending.

Function review: Types of questions

Open questions: often use the modal 'can'. Make sure you know the correct structure: **Can + verb. The verb 'explain' may also be used** A common error needs to be avoided: *Can you explain to me* **NOT** ~~explain me~~

Can you tell me a bit about + noun?   Can you tell me a bit about the pain?

Can you explain about +noun? Can you explain about the nausea you experience when you eat?

Can you explain to me how often you get muscle aches?

Closed questions: often use *Do you? / Are you? / Have you? / 'Wh'* questions

Do you + verb?   Do you have any serious medical problems?

Don't you + verb? Don't you realise how dangerous it is to mix your medications?

Are you + verb?   Are you allergic to anything?

Aren't you + verb? Aren't you doing any exercise at all?

Have you got any + noun? Have you got any questions?

Haven't you got any + noun? Haven't you got any health problems at all?

When do you + verb?   When do you notice the pain?

What do you... + verb?   What do you think about the weight loss plan?

Where is + noun? Where is the pain?

How do you...? How do you find the new medication?

Case Studies: Sleep Apnoea

Before you start think about vocab you may need to talk about sleep apnoea.

Talking about the breathing difficulties:

trouble breathing / problems with breathing

snoring / noisy breathing

insomnia / difficulty getting to sleep/difficulty staying asleep

Consequences of sleep apnoea

daytime tiredness / daytime sleepiness /suffer from fatigue

affects relationship with partner

Look at the role play cards below. Remember that you will only see your role play card (nurse) so you will have to guess what the patient will say to you. Look at the nurse's card first and think about how you will conduct the role play.

Some of the language used in the role play

Find out the history of the problem: Think of the sort of questions you need to ask:

How long have you had trouble sleeping?

When did your sleep problems start?

Talking about treatment - (use future tenses)

You'll go to the Sleep Clinic for assessment first.

You'll have to have an assessment at the Sleep Clinic.

You'll start on a weight loss plan to help you lose weight.

We'll give you a CPAP machine to use at night.

Explaining equipment

A CPAP machine is a device which has a mask like an oxygen mask.

The mask helps to increase pressure in the throat so that the airways do not collapse.

You put the mask on in the same way as an ordinary oxygen mask.

Giving advice:

It would be a good idea to try to lose some weight.

It may help if you could lose some weight.

It might help your breathing if you lost some weight.

The following advice is more serious advice so you use stronger phrases.

You should avoid taking medications which make you sleepy.

It's important not to drink too much alcohol.

Function review: Making suggestions /giving advice/saying what must happen

These functions range from the most 'gentle' (making a suggestion which the other person can choose to accept or not but the choice will not affect their health) to the 'informational' (giving advice so you know what will help you improve your health) to the 'essential' (saying what is essential to do to avoid problems).

Green

Have you thought about + ing?
What about + ing?
Why don't you try + ing?

Yellow

It would be a good idea to + verb. It's not a good idea to + verb.
It would be helpful to + verb. It's not helpful to + verb.
You should + verb. You shouldn't + verb.

Red

You must + verb.   You mustn't + verb.
It is essential that you + verb.
It's essential that you don't + verb.
Do not + verb.

Role play cards

Check the tasks which you, the nurse, will undertake.

Setting: Medical Centre

Nurse: You are a GP Practice Nurse who has been asked to talk to a 65 year-old patient about sleep apnoea. He is going to attend a Sleep Clinic for assessment but doesn't understand why. He is obese but not keen on losing weight. He also needs to use a CPAP machine (type of oxygen mask which keeps the airways open) but does not know much about it.

Task:

1. Find out the history of the problem.

2. Explain that the GP thinks he may have obstructive sleep apnoea. Explain the difference between snoring and sleep apnoea and why it can be a serious condition - e.g. extreme fatigue, increased risk of stroke and heart attack.

3. Outline the treatment which the GP has prescribed:

- assessment at the Sleep Clinic

- weight loss to reduce the pressure on his neck

- avoiding medications and alcohol which may make him sleepy

- use of a CPAP machine to keep the airways open at night.

Now, check the patient's card. Notice that the patient is going to raise an embarrassing problem – the patient is hinting that his sex life is being affected because he is sleeping in the spare room. How will you manage this? The patient is also reluctant to lose weight, although you know that this is very important in order to reduce the risks of sleep apnoea.

Setting: Medical Centre

Patient: You are a 65 year-old patient who has had problems snoring for several months. Your wife complains about your snoring and has started sleeping in the spare room. Now, the GP says it's sleep apnoea and you don't understand what this means.

Task:

1. Explain that you had a car accident 6 months ago and you had injuries to your nose. Since then you have been snoring. You wake up very tired every morning.

2. You are a bit embarrassed about your wife sleeping in the spare room and are worried that your marriage is going to suffer unless you fix the problem.

3. You find it hard to lose weight and are not sure that it is

---

important anyway.

6. Explaining a procedure

In order to explain a procedure during a role play there are several factors to think about.

• Use everyday language rather than medical terminology where possible. Assume that your patient doesn't have or has limited knowledge of medical procedures.

• Try to structure the explanation in steps of no more than three parts. This way you can use **signposting terms** like *Firstly, secondly, lastly.* You can prepare explanations and practise them before the test. Think about the sort of things you are likely to need to explain to a patient and the vocab you might need.
For example,

- a dressing for a burn

- how to look after a dressing including removal of stitches

- pain relief after an operation

- the need for a medication (antibiotic, tetanus injection, immunisation)

- reason for a blood test

- Include clarifying language to ensure that you understand what the patient has said. This also shows that you are listening carefully to the patient.

VOCAB – Wounds and dressings

When you are writing	When you are speaking
a lesion (She has a lesion on her forearm.)	a sore
a laceration	a cut
an ulcer	an ulcer
incision line	surgical cut
a burn / a scald / a chemical burn	a burn / a scald or a steam burn / a chemical burn
a vesicle	a blister
a haematoma	a collection of blood under the skin
a contusion / an ecchymosis	a bruise
have a dressing done Mrs X had her dressing done before discharge.	to do a dressing I'm going to do your dressing.
dressing attended (in the patient notes)	The dressing has been done.
leave the wound open	leave the wound open I'm going to leave the wound open.

leave the wound intact	not take the dressing off
have the wound sutured	You're going to need some stitches.
have the sutures /clips removed	You have to have your stitches out.
remove the sutures in 7-10 days	take out the stitches in 7 to 10 days.
had sutures /clips inserted during the operation	had the stitches / put in during the operation
review the dressing	see how the dressing is going / see what the dressing is like
monitor the wound and check for infection	keep an eye on
clean / cleanse the wound	clean the wound
clean the ulcer	clean the ulcer
apply a non-adhesive dressing	put on a non-stick dressing
attach the dressing with surgical tape	I'm going to tape on the dressing.
secure the dressing with a bandage	keep the dressing in place with a bandage
apply cream to the burn	put some cream on the burn
apply the ointment to the incision line	put some ointment onto the surgical cut
the wound is granulating well	the wound is healing well.

Case study: Dog bite

The dog bite role play contains several explanations. You need to explain about the dressing to the bite, lack of sutures and the need for a tetanus jab. This role play differs from other role plays in that the nurse has to explain why sutures are **not needed.** Check the language used to explain these things.

Explaining what is NOT going to be done.

You won't need any sutures /stitches.

You won't have to have sutures. / stitches.

It's best to / It's better to....leave the wound open

Persuading

Notice that the patient is reluctant to have a tetanus jab. The patient keeps insisting that s/he doesn't think it is really important to have the injection. How are you going to persuade the patient?

Before you try to explain why the injection is important, you need to empathise with the patient, so that the patient knows that you appreciate why s/he may not want to have the tetanus jab. Then try to explain the importance of the tetanus jab (prevents tetanus which is a dangerous illness)

The Role play cards

Setting: An Emergency Ward

Nurse: You are attending to a woman who has sustained a dog bite. She was brought to hospital by her friend. The wound will not need to be sutured but she will need a tetanus shot.

Task:

1. Find out as much as you can about the dog bite – How did it happen? Where is the bite?

2. Explain what treatment will be given – clean the wound, it won't need sutures because the wound must be left open, after that, a clean dressing. Keep wound clean and dry at home.

3. Find out about the patient's last tetanus jab? Explain that she will have to have a tetanus jab now .Persuade her that it is essential that she has the jab – dog bites cause dirty wounds, high risk of developing tetanus.

    4. Agree to get some pain killers. She can take some home as well for the next two days. Suggest she rests her leg when she can.

Setting: An Emergency Ward

Patient: You were bitten by a dog and have a painful wound. You were brought to hospital by a friend who was with you at the time.

Task:

1. Tell the nurse about your accident (you were walking to a friend's house when a dog rushed up and bit your leg. It's a very deep gash on your right lower leg. It is still bleeding a lot and is very painful.

2. Ask why she won't have sutures – how will the wound heal?

3. Explain last tetanus jab 12 years ago. You don't want one – it's only a dog bite. You really hate injections. Finally agree to have the jab.

4. Ask if you can have something for the pain. It stings a lot especially when she walks.

Nurse: [Introduce yourself]

Hello. My name is _____. I'm one of the nurses here.

Nurse: [Ask what happened]

Can you tell me ……..?

Patient: I was walking to my friend's house when a dog rushed up and bit my leg. I was just about to open the gate to her house when the dog ran up.

Nurse: [Ask where the bite is]

Right, I see. Can you tell me …….?

Patient: It's on my right leg. You can see the gash on my lower leg. It's really deep. I'm afraid it's still bleeding. It's a bit of a mess.

Nurse: That's OK. **[Explain what you are going to do]**

I'll just explain what I'll do now. First, (clean the wound)

The bite won't need any sutures (stitches)

After that, (a clean dressing)

Patient: OK, I see. It is very deep. Why no stitches?

Nurse: [Explain wound must be open]

 We don't suture dog bites.

It's better to leave the wound open.

Patient: All right. I see. Is there anything else I have to do?

Nurse: [Advise keep wound clean and dry]

You need to…………… (keep clean and dry)

Try not to ……… when you have a shower.

Patient: OK. I'll be careful.

Nurse: [Find out about last tetanus jab]

Can you tell me when …………………

Patient: Oh! It must have been around 12 years ago.

Nurse: [Explain she must have a tetanus jab]

You'll have to have

It's very important.

Patient: Oh look.. I really don't want an injection. I hate them.

And, it's only a dog bite – it's probably clean under all the blood.

Nurse: [Persuade patient it is essential to have the tetanus jab]

It really is ……………………….

Dog bites are actually very dirty. And you need to protect yourself

against tetanus.

Patient: All right, I suppose I should have it. Could I also have

some painkillers? It still stings a lot especially when I walk.

Nurse: [Say you'll get some now]

Sure, I'll …………..

Offer to get some to take home]

I'll get you……….

[Suggest what to do at home – put legs up and rest]

It would be a good idea to …

Case study: diabetic amputation

Look at the role play cards below and think about the language functions you may need to use. Review some possible language functions that you might use.

Have a look at these examples. Remember that you do not have to be medically accurate. So, you don't have to explain things like the type of solution you will use to clean the wound etc. You just have to explain the procedures in a simple way. If you are not sure about the procedure, explain it in a general way. Look at these examples:

1. IV antibiotics

You'll have some IV antibiotics. 'IV' just means 'in the vein'.
We'll give you the antibiotics through a drip in your arm.
I'll put the antibiotics into the drip in your arm.

2. Dressing

I'm going to change your dressing. I'll clean the wound then I'll put on a clean dressing. I'll put on a bandage too to keep the dressing place.

3. Doing a blood sugar test

First, prick your finger and put a drop of blood on the test strip. Then put the test strip in the glucometer (or 'testing machine', if you can't remember the correct name) . Wait until you see the result on the screen.

4. Using a PCA

You'll have a small button connected to a drip. If you have any pain, press the button and you will get a dose of painkiller. You don't have to worry about getting too much medication, there is a lock-out function.

Hint: Prepare some possible dialogues which you may use to explain common procedures, e.g.

* giving a painkiller
* giving an IV e.g. IV antibiotic
* doing a dressing
* giving an injection e.g. a vaccination
* doing a blood test /getting a blood test result
* taking a urine specimen e.g. for a UTI

Explaining that you don't know the answer to a question.

For example, the patient asks about the possibility of an amputation. The nurse empathises first by saying 'I understand that it is very difficult for you' then she explains that the patient needs to speak to the doctor.

It's not a good idea to say 'I don't know about that' Much better to say that you appreciate how hard it is but it would be better to speak to the doctor about that. This way you are demonstrating that you can empathise and make suggestions.

Watch a sample video of this dialogue at
www.youtube.com/watch?v=wrL_ARTZPyw
Transcript:
Nurse: Hello my name is Soraya. I'm one of the nurses here in A&E. Do you mind if I call you Libby?

Patient: Oh, hello. That's fine.

Nurse: I see from your notes that you have a cut on your foot. Is that right?

Patient: Yes. That's right. I've got a cut on my little toe, on my right foot.

Nurse: OK. Can you tell me a bit about what happened? How did you get the cut?

Patient: Sure. Look, I wouldn't have worried except that I'm diabetic. I'm usually so careful. I went to the beach with some friends and we were walking a bit too close to the rocks. I slipped on a rock and cut my foot.

Nurse: I see. When did you cut yourself?

Patient: It was yesterday. I was at the beach in the morning. I cut my foot just before lunch. I tried to clean the cut in salt water and I put on a bandaid as well. I thought that would be enough.

Nurse: Uh huh. Can you tell me a bit more about what happened this morning?

Patient: Well, when I woke up I noticed that my toe was red and swollen. It just didn't look right. That's why I came here. I'm worried now that the cut is infected.

Nurse: You did the right thing coming to hospital as soon as possible. It's very important for diabetics to seek medical help quickly if they have a cut or a wound. Wound infections can develop quickly if you are not careful.

Patient: Yes, I thought so. The problem is that it isn't painful. If I hadn't checked my toe this morning, I would never have known that there was a problem.

Nurse: Yes. It can be very difficult. It's always important to be careful if you have an injury. If you have high blood sugar levels it can damage the nerves in your feet. That's the reason why you might lose some feeling in your toes and you might not be able to feel any pain. You should check your feet every day for any small cuts to prevent infections from developing.

Patient: I know, I am usually very careful with my feet. This morning I started getting worried about my toe especially when I saw how red it was. I even looked it up on the internet. There's another thing. I was reading about diabetic amputations. Now I'm terrified in case I end up losing my toe. They won't do that, will they?

Nurse: I understand that you're very worried but it's best to wait and talk to the doctor about that. You'll have a surgical consultation this afternoon. The surgical consultant is a specialist doctor who will explain any surgery you might need to have. Amputations are only needed if a diabetic infection doesn't heal. You came to hospital promptly so we can treat the infection quickly. I know it is difficult but you will have to wait until this afternoon and have a chat with the specialist.

Patient: Oh OK. I see. So, you're saying that it might not be necessary.

Nurse: That's right. I know it's very worrying for you at the moment but I'm afraid that I can't give you any more information about surgery until you speak to the specialist. However, I can explain what will happen now. The first thing is that you'll have some IV antibiotics to clear up any infection. IV just means 'in the vein'. The antibiotics are very strong so we give them through the drip in your arm. They can get into your blood-stream more quickly then.

Patient: OK. Someone just put a drip in my arm. That's what it's for, is it?

Nurse: Yes. We'll give you IV antibiotics for a couple of days. It's important to treat the infection as soon as possible. The next thing is to look at the cut and do the dressing. I'll clean the wound and put on a new dressing. Then I'll put on a bandage to hold the dressing in place. I'll give you a special boot to use when you are walking. It will protect your toe from being knocked.

Patient: So I shouldn't use a bandaid to cover the cut?

Nurse: No, it would be better to use the special dressings that I'll give you to take home. When you go home you should change the dressing every two days. I can show you how to do the dressing and I'll give you some dressings to take home with you. If you can't manage it yourself, can make arrangements for the community nurse to come and do it for you.

Patient: I see. If you show me how to do the dressing I'll see if I can manage. Ah..You said something about a boot. Sorry, I forgot what you said.

Nurse: That's all right. It is a lot to take in. What I said was that I would change your dressing and then give you a protective boot to wear. The boot has a soft lining so your foot is protected from anything that is sharp. You need to wear it until your toe has healed completely.

Patient: OK. I understand now. Is there anything else I need to do?

Nurse: No, not at the moment. I'll show you how to do the dressing now. I also have a leaflet here for you about foot care for diabetics. It will explain some of the things I have been talking about. If you have any questions after you read it just let me know. OK?

Patient: Yes. Thank you. That would be very helpful.

7. Giving advice and making suggestions

Think about the times when you may need to give advice.

* before a patient is discharged home (advice about dressings, removal of sutures)

* before taking a new medication

* using a piece of equipment (CPAP machine, nebuliser)

* making lifestyle changes (weight loss, quit smoking, increasing exercise)

What about making suggestions? A suggestion may follow a piece of advice. You may be helping the patient to see ways that s/he can follow your advice, e.g.

* starting to exercise more by taking a short walk at first with a friend.

* setting a realistic goal of the number of cigarettes to be smoked each day in decreasing numbers

* starting a diet diary to note down all the food which is eaten each day to pin point problem areas in the diet.

Giving advice about sensitive topics

There are some topics which are quite difficult to advise on, e.g. reducing alcohol consumption which is excessive, the need for incontinence aids, unsightly scars. As with persuading, it is important to first acknowledge that it may be embarrassing for the patient to discuss the problem. *I understand that it might be difficult for you to talk about this but it is very important that I give you some information.*

Giving advice or making suggestions when the patient is reluctant

What can you do if the patient refuses your advice or is reluctant to follow your suggestions? Always remembering that patients have the right to accept or refuse advice, try to think of ways that you can persuade the patient to accept at least part of your advice.

Would you be willing to try to cut down smoking a little? (the patient has said s/he doesn't want to give up smoking at the moment)

Case study - Irritable Bowel Syndrome

First, review the vocab you may need to talk about IBS.

Intestinal problems / digestive disorder

flare-up of symptoms / symptoms come and go

excess wind / flatulence / abdominal bloating

stomach cramps

gas-producing food

anti-diarrhoeals / anti diarrhoea medication

laxatives / constipation medication

pain relief

anti-spasmodic medications / anti stomach cramps

This role play allows you to demonstrate these language functions:

1. Asking about the frequency of symptoms

How often have you had the symptoms?

How many times a year do you have the symptoms?

How frequent are the bouts of IBS?

2. Asking about the duration of symptoms

How long do the symptoms last?

3. Asking about the type of pain

What does it feel like when you have the bouts of IBS?

What type of pain do you get?

What is the pain like?

4. Giving advice to a patient with IBS

You need to take the tablets when you have any pain?

You should use the tablets to control the symptoms.

It would be a good idea to make some dietary changes.

You might like to think about eliminating high fibre foods from your diet.

It's advisable to avoid gas-producing foods like cabbage.

Try to avoid stressful situations if you can.

5. Confirming information

So, what you're saying is that you have episodes of diarrhoea and abdominal cramps around three times a year?

What I understand is that you have these bouts of abdominal bloating every month. Is that right?

Can I just check what you are saying? You mentioned that you have episodes of diarrhoea and constipation every few week. Is that correct?

Setting: Gastroenterology Clinic

Nurse: You are the nurse who works at the Gastroenterology Clinic. You see patients after they undergo tests at the clinic. You are now talking to Jenny Vassily, a 25 year-old who has been diagnosed with Irritable Bowel Syndrome at the clinic. The patient is not sure about the condition and needs advice about treatment and management.

Task:

1. Find out about the symptoms she experiences e.g. type, duration, frequency, pain.

2. Find out about any triggers she may have noticed – e.g. stress

3. Explain what IBS is in simple language - no clear cause but intestines probably oversensitive at times, smooth muscle becomes overactive – spasms, cramps, IBS - either constipation, diarrhoea or both.

4. Outline treatment options – pt has been supplied with medication for pain, diarrhoea and constipation. She needs to make diet changes (avoid high fibre foods and gas-producing foods like cabbage, eat regular meals). Stress management – suggest activities like yoga, meditation or gentle walks.

Setting: Gastroenterology Clinic

Patient: You are a 25 year-old who has just received a diagnosis of IBS. You had a colonoscopy early this week at the clinic. You have had several episodes of abdominal cramps, flatulence and diarrhoea. It's been very embarrassing as you did not know what to do about the symptoms.

Task :

1. You have had some episodes of painful abdominal cramps, frequent wind problems, which are very embarrassing, and bowel problems. It started about 3 months ago – you have had bouts of diarrhoea and constipation. It has happened a few times. You have been off your food. You feel bloated and uncomfortable. It is actually very painful when it happens.

2. You have noticed that it was worse a few months ago as you had a lot of stress at that time. You started a new job which is highly paid but very stressful.

3. You've heard the name before, IBS, but you don't know

anything about it. You thought it meant that you were allergic to fibre in food.

4. You understand about the tablets now. Check that you only take the tablets if you have cramps, diarrhoea or vomiting. Confirm that the other suggestions, diet changes and stress management, are things she should do all the time to try to prevent future bouts of the condition.

You can read the transcript of a suggested dialogue below watch the video on YouTube at

www.youtube.com/watch?v=sJ0ghw_TPV8

Nurse: Hello Jenny. Thanks for coming to see me. My name is Sarah. I'm the Clinic Nurse at the Gastroenterology Clinic.

Patient: Hello, Sarah. Thanks for talking to me today.

Nurse: That's OK. I see that you have had some tests at the clinic and that you've been diagnosed with Irritable Bowel Syndrome. Is that right?

Patient: Yes, that's right. I had a test and now they are saying that it's

IBS. Irritable Bowel Syndrome. I don't really know much about it.

Nurse: I see. Yes, it is a lot to take in at once. I'll explain what happens with the condition in a minute but I'd like to ask you a few questions first. Is that all right?

Patient: Yes. That's fine.

Nurse: Can you tell me what's been happening with your bowels?

Patient: Well, uhm... I have this awful abdominal pain. It's like a colicky pain in my stomach. Uhm...and it's actually really embarrassing because I keep passing wind and I keep going to the toilet as well.

Nurse: Mm. It must have been very difficult for you. Can I just confirm with you that you've had a lot of abdominal pain and diarrhoea and you've also had a problem with wind. Is that right?

Patient: Yes, it is. It doesn't happen all the time. But when it happens, it's very painful.

Nurse: OK. You mentioned that you have diarrhoea from time to time. Is it only diarrhoea or constipation as well?

Patient: What do you mean? You have to have either diarrhoea or constipation, don't you?

Nurse: Not necessarily. There are a few different types of IBS. Some people just have constipation and some people have diarrhoea. Other people have both together which is very unpleasant.

Patient: Oh, right. No, I just have diarrhoea but, as I said before, it's not all the time.

Nurse: OK, I see. So, it's just diarrhoea. How often do you have the diarrhoea?

Patient: Well, I've had three or four bouts so far. I get terrible cramps as well.

Nurse: And, how long have you had these symptoms?

Patient: I've had the problem for around three months. Ah, yes, it started around three months ago.

Nurse: Right. I'll explain now what happens when you have IBS. Basically, irritable bowel syndrome is a digestive condition which causes uncomfortable bowel symptoms. People may have loose, mushy stools when they go to the toilet. I mean, when they have a bowel movement. Alternatively, they might have hard stools and strain when they go to the toilet.

Patient: Do they know what causes it?

Nurse: No. They don't know the exact cause. That's why it is different from other bowel conditions. The structure of the intestines is quite normal but the intestines appear to be over sensitive at some times. That's what gives you the bloating and intestinal spasms.

Patient: I see. Yes, I get bloating a lot. What about my diet? The doctor mentioned something might be wrong with my diet.

Nurse: Yes. That's right. There are certain foods which make the condition worse. Can you tell me what your diet is like? What kind of foods do you tend to eat?

Patient: Actually, I always thought that I had a good diet. You know, I try to eat a lot of vegetables and I like whole grain bread. I thought that was the best thing to do but now I don't know what I should eat.

Nurse: A small amount of fibre in your diet is important to keep your bowels moving properly. But, you will need to cut out high fibre foods if you can. It's a good idea to increase the amount of water that you drink as well.

Patient: OK. Is the fibre in my diet giving me the bloating?

Nurse: No, that tends to be from gas-producing foods like cabbage, for example. I'll give you a patient information leaflet on the foods which you should avoid to make it easier for you. Then you can try to avoid foods which cause you problems.

Patient: I see. They told me that my intestine was normal after the colonoscopy so it was a bit confusing.

Nurse: The problem is that the intestines in IBS are overly sensitive and this seems to result in either constipation or diarrhoea. Some people report that there are things which trigger bouts of IBS. You mentioned that your symptoms started around three months ago. Can you think of anything which was happening at that time?

Patient: Yes. I started a new job around then. It was really stressful especially at first. I have a lot of responsibility and I work long hours too.

Nurse: I see. So what you are saying is that the symptoms seemed to coincide with your new job?

Patient: Uhm, yes. I suppose they did. Could that have something to do with getting IBS?

Nurse: Yes, it could be part of the reasons why you started having the episodes of bowel problems. When you feel tense and you can't relax, it can affect your bowels.

Patient: Oh, I see.

Nurse: So apart from watching your diet and avoiding high fibre and gas-producing foods, it's a good idea to think about some ways that you can reduce the stress in your life. Yoga and meditation are good ways to reduce stress. Have you ever tried either of these?

Patient: No and to be honest, I don't think I'd like to. They don't appeal to me at all.

Nurse: OK. What about going for a walk after work?

Patient: Well, that sounds a bit better. It doesn't sound very relaxing to me though.

Nurse: If you listen to some calming music as you walk it can be quite relaxing. Would you be willing to try it? It really is a good idea to learn to relax as it has a positive effect on IBS. Especially after a stressful day at work.

Patient: OK. I'll give it a try. Anything to stop those awful cramps.

Nurse: That's great. I'll give you the leaflet about IBS now. Try to go for some gentle walks and see if that helps you. There is a phone number on the leaflet for the IBS Support group. You may find that helpful too.

Patient: Right, thanks. That might be very useful.

Case Study – Eczema

Before you start, think of the vocab you may need to discuss eczema.

dry out / be very dry

itchy

scratch

blistery / have blisters

skin condition

cream / ointment /moisturiser

weeping /discharge

Patient Information Leaflets

Patient information leaflets are found in all hospital areas. They are produced to help patients and their relatives understand medical conditions and medical treatment. The leaflets may also contain phone numbers of support groups which patients or their relatives may find helpful.

You can also use patient information leaflets at the end of the role play. When you are rounding off the conversation you can offer the patient a leaflet and suggest that they read about the things you have been discussing. They can call the number on the leaflet if they have any questions.

Talking about things which are essential (not suggestions)
It's essential that you put on the moisturising cream several times a day.
It is extremely important that she takes all the antibiotics.
Make sure that she has the antibiotics with some food.

Look at the nurse's role play card. The patient information leaflet follows.

Setting: Accident and Emergency

Nurse: You are talking to a woman who has brought in her 18 month old daughter who has been scratching almost constantly and barely sleeps. Her daughter has eczema; the GP prescribed steroid creams and moisturisers but the patient is worried about using them. There are weeping areas on the little girl's arms which look infected. That's why the patient came in today.

Task:

1.   Find out as much as you can about the eczema - when does it happen? Where is the rash?

2.   Ask about triggers e.g. soap and detergent, woollen clothing, dairy products and eggs.

3.   Explain about eczema –The cause is not known but it seems to be liked with allergies.

4.   Explain the importance of using the creams – important to moisturise the skin. Steroids are only needed flare ups or acute episodes – they are safe to use for short periods of time – reduces itching.

5.   Explain that the mother has done the right thing coming in –

if areas with eczema become infected, the child may need antibiotics. It's important to see the GP in the future if infection is suspected.

6. Give the mother a leaflet with advice about the changes in care which may help (use the leaflet to help you)

Patient leaflet

Helpful hints to manage eczema

1. A comfortable bed

* Don't over heat the bedroom – a cool temperature is more comfortable

* Bed linen should be cotton or natural fibres – wool can make itching worse

* Apply moisturising cream before bedtime – let the cream sink in

2. Don't use perfumed soaps or shampoos

 * Avoid soaps which dry out the skin – use special oils or water

* Avoid washing too often – it strips natural oils from the skin

* Wash in warm water rather than hot water

3. Use moisturising creams and steroid creams when prescribed

* Keep skin soft and moist – moisturised skin less likely to become infected

* Steroids prescribed for small inflamed areas – not the same as anabolic

steroids used by weight lifters

4. Help your child to stop scratching

* scratching may lead to bleeding and infected skin

* keep finger nails short

* distract your child if she is scratching a lot

5. Look at diet triggers

* food like dairy products e.g. milk, eggs, citrus fruit, chocolate, peanuts and

colourings may trigger eczema

Patient's role play card

Setting: Accident and Emergency

Patient: You have brought in your 18 month old daughter who has been scratching almost constantly and barely sleeps. It is making you very tired too. Your daughter has eczema and the GP has prescribed steroid creams and moisturisers for the eczema. You don't want to use the steroid cream because you have read all about steroids. You daughter's arms look infected and you don't know what to put on them.

Task:

1. The eczema started when your daughter was about 6 months old. When she stopped breast-feeding and started drinking regular milk. Orange juice affects your daughter as well. Rash worse when you use perfumed soap. Rash very noticeable behind the knees.

2. Triggers seem to be dairy and orange juice. Also a perfumed soap which you avoid now.

3. Be unconvinced about steroids – aren't they used by weight builders?

4. Ask the nurse to explain about the antibiotics again. You can't remember what the nurse said.

5. Tell the nurse that the information in the leaflet is useful.

Watch the sample video at

http://www.youtube.com/watch?v=kvVdzZX18kY **and follow the**

transcript below.

Nurse: Hello, I'm George. I'm one of the nurses in A&E. I've looked at your daughter's notes and I see that she has eczema.

Patient: Yes. That's right.

Nurse: Can you tell me about your daughter's eczema? What happens when she has eczema?

Patient: Look it's awful. It started when she was about 6 months old. She just scratches most of the time. She finds it hard to sleep she scratches so much.

Nurse: I see. Yes, it is very unpleasant. Where does she have the eczema?

Patient: It's mainly behind her knees. She also has a rash in her elbows. The problem is that it's easy to scratch there.

Nurse: Yes, it is. Have you noticed anything that starts it off? Anything that triggers it?

Patient: Yes. I was thinking about the things which might make it worse. I think it started when she stopped breast feeding. As soon as she started drinking milk she got the rash. I'm not sure but I think orange juice makes it worse too.

Nurse: Well, both those things are common triggers. We can talk about things to avoid later. I've got some information for you.

Patient: That would be very helpful. I try to do things to help her but I'm not really sure about eczema at all. I don't even know what causes it.

Nurse: They are not sure what causes it actually. It seems to be linked with allergies. Particularly allergies to foods like dairy products and citrus.

Patient: That makes sense. She can't drink milk or orange juice. Fortunately, she likes drinking other types of juice.

Nurse: Some children are sensitive to wool and do better if they only wear cotton. There are several other common allergies which are linked to eczema. For example, pet allergies seem to go hand in hand with eczema.

Patient: Yes, I remember reading about that on the internet.

Nurse: Can you tell me about your daughter's current treatment? Does she use creams on the eczema?

Patient: Yes. Well, sometimes. The GP gave me some cream to use every day. It's like a moisturiser.

Nurse: That's good. It's very important to use the moisturiser a few times a day. When do you usually put the cream on?

Patient: I put it on first thing in the morning after she has a bath. Then a couple of times during the day if she is itching a lot. I try to put it on last thing at night. Before she goes to bed.

Nurse: It sounds like you are doing the right thing with the moisturiser. Can you just tell me again about her bath-time. How often do you give your daughter a bath?

Patient: I give her a bath every morning so she is clean for the day. I use special soap, not perfumed soap.

Nurse: OK. I understand. It might be better for the eczema if your daughter did not have a bath every day. Baths tend to dry out the skin.

Patient: Even if I use a moisturiser afterwards?

Nurse: That's right. Try to wipe her hands and face with a moist cloth instead. Can you tell me about any other creams you are using?

Patient: Well, I'm supposed to use a steroid cream if her skin gets very red and inflamed. The thing is that I don't want to use the steroid cream. I don't think it's safe.

Nurse: I can appreciate your concerns. Many people worry about steroid creams because they think it's like the steroids that weight lifters use.

Patient: Yes, that's what I thought.

Nurse: No, the cream that your GP suggested that you use is a very low dose of steroid medication. You only use the cream when her eczema flares up. It's only a short-term treatment.

Patient: I'm still not happy about it. I've been reading about some natural creams which are supposed to be good.

Nurse: I think I know the ones you mean. Some of these creams can be helpful but it's important to remember that they are still medications. Your GP has prescribed a cream that she thinks is right for your daughter. And only to be used now and then when the condition gets worse. We need to stop your daughter itching so much that her skin bleeds.

Patient: Oh dear, maybe that's why it happened! Her skin became very red and extremely itchy last week. She was scratching all the time. Then some of the areas on both her arms started to bleed. Now they are weepy and I'm worried that it's infected.

Nurse: You did the right thing coming in. If it is infected, your daughter will be put on some antibiotics.

Patient: I see. OK, some antibiotics.

Nurse: It is extremely important that she takes all the antibiotics. Also, make sure that she has the antibiotics with some food. You could give her the antibiotics with a biscuit or a piece of toast.

Patient: That's a good idea. I'll try that.

Nurse: Right, I'll give you this patient information leaflet now. We can go through the hints together.

Patient: Oh yes. This is very helpful.

Nurse: Try to keep your daughter cool especially at night. That may make it easier for her to sleep at night. It would also be better to dress your daughter in clothes made of cotton or natural fibres.

Patient: OK. That makes sense. I'll try to keep her room a bit cooler.

Nurse: Try to cut down on the number of baths your daughter has. I remember that you said that you use special soap to wash your daughter. That's good. It's essential that you put on the moisturising cream several times a day. Keeping the skin moisturised is one way you can help to prevent skin infections.

Patient: OK. So, putting on the cream is very important.

Nurse: Yes, it is. Using the steroid cream if necessary is also very important. I'll just repeat the important information that using steroid cream is not the same as using the steroids that body builders use.

Patient: Yes, I understand that now. I can see that there are times when my daughter may need the steroid cream.

Nurse: That's great. There are some hints in the leaflet to help with the itching. Keep your daughter's finger nails short so she can't herself if she scratches. It's a good idea to take her mind off it, if she is starting to scratch.

Patient: Yeah. Sometimes she scratches herself very badly. I'll try those hints and see if it helps.

Nurse: The last hint is a reminder of the food triggers of eczema. You already know that your daughter is sensitive to dairy and citrus juices. Just keep an eye on any other foods which cause any problems.

Patient: I'll do that. Thank you for the advice. I'll take this leaflet home with me too.

8. Empathising and reassuring

There is a clear difference between sympathy and empathy. Sympathy is a close feeling of sorrow felt for the other person. Nurses who feel sympathetic about a patient's situations become overwhelmed by their feelings and are not able to maintain professional boundaries. They may also identify with the sad event on a personal level.

 On the other hand, empathy is the ability to imagine the sadness or distress a patient may be feeling. Empathetic responses indicate that you are trying to feel and understand something of what the other person is experiencing whilst retaining personal boundaries.

Steps in listening empathetically

Firstly, observe what the patient is experiencing and try to understand how a patient may feel when they experience these things. Then, try to identify what the patient may need.

Reassuring

Case study: BURNS

The burns role play is an example of a role play between a nurse and a patient's relative. In general, the scenarios involve a situation which is distressing to the relative, e.g.

*a young mother with a baby who may be jaundiced

*a grandmother who is anxious about her grandson's epilepsy

*a mother who is concerned about whether to vaccinate her child or not

*a mother with a child who is being admitted to hospital for the first time

Imagine how the patient's mother may be feeling. The mother may:

- be very upset
- feel guilty because she left her daughter unsupervised in the kitchen
- be worried about possible scarring
- want information and advice about First Aid and care at home

The nurse may have to:

- calm her - ask her to slow down / repeat information

- reassure that did the right thing

- explain what might happen /about treatment

- give advice about follow up care

Before you start, review terms which relate to burns in children.

scald / burn

accidental

scar /scarring

first degree burn / second degree burn / third degree burn

Examples of language used in the role play.

Calming a patient or relative: often best achieved by taking the person to a quiet area and helping them to relax by slowing their speech.

I know you're upset but I can't follow what you're saying. Can you tell me again?

Come and sit over here so we can have a talk. (taking the patient somewhere private)

Are you OK to talk about it now? (asking if it is a good time to talk)

Asking what happened?

Can you tell me what happened?

Can you tell me how your daughter burned herself?

Can you tell me how your daughter got burned?

How did your daughter get the burns?

Ask her to slow down

Could you slow down a bit. I can't follow what you're saying.

Could you speak a bit more slowly? I'm having trouble following what you're saying.

Repeat information

Can you repeat that last bit – I didn't quite catch it.

Can you tell me what you said again, I didn't understand it.

Explaining possible symptoms / after effects.

She might have some scarring.

She might have to use some cream for a few weeks to treat the burns.

It's possible that she may have some scarring but there are good treatments now.

There's a chance that she may have a bit of scarring.

Reassuring

I understand that you are very upset. Try not to worry too much, you did the right thing.

I appreciate how hard this is but you shouldn't be too concerned; you couldn't have done more.

I know it's very difficult but you did the right thing so try not to worry.

Follow up information

I'll explain about what you need to do when you go home.

You'll need to bathe her arm in mild soapy water.

Just apply a thin layer of cream to the burns then put on a non-adhesive dressing.

Make sure you put on a bandage from her wrist to her upper arm to keep the dressing on.

I have a patient information leaflet here with some information for you.

You can find the Emergency number at the bottom of the leaflet.

Read the role play cards below. The transcript of a sample YouTube video follows.

Setting: Emergency Department

Nurse: You are talking to a mother who has brought her 3 year-old daughter to A&E with burns to the left arm following an accident at home.

Task:

1. Find out as much as you can about the accident.

2. Reassure the parent that she used correct First Aid and that it is a very common accident to happen.

3. Explain what will to be done to treat the burns in hospital. You will give her daughter an injection or pain relief. Explain that the burns are second degree burns and there may be some scarring but it will fade in time.

4. Reassure the mother that everything will be ok. You can arrange further advice from a dermatologist if needed.

Setting: Emergency Department

Patient: You have brought in your 3 year old daughter with burns to the left arm following an accident at home. You are very distressed.

Task:

1. Explain how the accident occurred - you were cooking dinner when your child pulled a saucepan with hot water on herself. You took her shirt off and put it under cold water then applied it to the burn. You are not sure if you have done the right thing or not.

2. You feel so guilty that your child will have permanent scarring to her arm; all because you answered the telephone and left your daughter in the kitchen.

3. Ask what to do if it happens again. Make sure you know how to look after the burns when your daughter goes home.

Now, watch the video on YouTube at

https://www.youtube.com/watch?v=j_YSX6Fvbsg

Dialogue: Child with burns

Nurse: Hello. It's Mrs Smith, isn't it? I believe your daughter got burnt last night. Can you tell me how it happened?

Patient's mother: I was cooking dinner last night. I was busy, you know. I got distracted. I shouldn't have done it. I know I should have taken more care. The phone rang and I went out of the kitchen to answer it.

Nurse: That's OK. Take it slowly. I want to make sure I understand correctly. So you were cooking dinner last night and what happened then?

Patient's mother: I was cooking rice and my daughter wanted to see what I was doing. She wanted to see how much rice I was cooking. That's when she tipped the hot water on herself. And when she burned herself.

Nurse: I see. That must have been very frightening for you. And for your daughter.

Patient's mother: It was awful. It happened so fast too.

Nurse: Yes, it can happen very fast. Can you tell me what you did first, you know, to do something about the burns?

Patient's mother: All I could think of was to take my daughter's shirt off and soak it in cold water. I put the wet shirt over the burns on her arm. Did I do the right thing? I just did what I thought was right.

Nurse: Yes, you did the right thing. People used to put butter on burns but it's the worst thing you can do. You made the right choice.

Patient's mother: But I feel so guilty. Look at her arms. She'll have terrible scars.

Nurse: I know it looks awful now but it will look a lot better when the burns start to heal. You must try not to feel guilty. Children at this age are very inquisitive. They just want to look at everything but they don't realise the dangers. Scalds on the arms especially the hands and fingers are very common. And the scalds most often happen in the kitchen.

Patient's mother: But I shouldn't have answered the phone! If only I had stayed in the kitchen. I don't know. I feel so bad.

Nurse: I understand that you feel bad about the accident but I think it important to focus on what we are going to do now to treat the burns. Is that OK?

Patient's mother: Oh yes. Sorry. What happens now? What are you going to do? She's in a lot of pain.

Nurse: Yes, I know. So the first thing I'll do is to give her a small injection to help with the pain. When the pain is under control I'm going to wash her arm very gently and put on some special cream. The cream will help stop any infection to the burned area. We also need to make sure she is drinking enough. Can you help with that?

Patient's mother: Yes, sure. I'll give her sips of water whenever I can.

Nurse: That's great.

Patient's mother: I'm sorry, I don't think I took in what you said about the scarring. Can you tell me again, please?

Nurse: Sure. It's a lot to take in. What I said was that it looks bad now because her skin is very red. It will look better once the skin starts to heal. Your daughter will need to have dressings to the burns when she goes home. I'll give you a follow-up appointment for the Dressings clinic. They may arrange for a community nurse to come to your house after a few clinic visits.

Patient's mother: OK. That sounds OK. I'm still a worried about the scarring. Is there anything I can do about it?

Nurse: After the burn has healed the clinic will probably refer your daughter to a dermatologist. There are some very good treatments these days so please try not to worry too much. I know it is difficult to remember everything so you might find this brochure helpful. It has some advice on making your home as safe as possible to avoid accidents.

Patient's mother: I see. OK well that makes me feel a bit better. Thank you.

Nurse: That's all right. Read through the brochure and ask us if you still have any questions. There is a contact number at the bottom of the brochure.

Grammar Focus: Using past tenses

Review the use of the past tenses:

Past simple: most often used to tell a story (called a narrative tense).

used for a completed action in the past

used with 'ago' e.g. *I moved to Sydney 6 months ago.*

used with *'in [a year]'* e.g. *I went to Singapore in 1976.*

Past continuous: for actions which were continuous or which took place a long time.

used to explain an action which was happening at the time of another action e.g. *I was going down the stairs when I tripped over.*

often seen with 'when' or 'while' e.g. *When I was walking along the street...., While I was cooking dinner...*

'Used to' : used for past habits

e.g. *I used to drink coffee at night but I don't now.*

9. Persuading

Sometimes during the role play your 'patient' will try to make it a bit more difficult for you. The patient, as in authentic situations, may be resistant to making changes which will benefit their health.

These changes might relate to:

* lifestyle changes (smoking, exercise)
* dietary changes (eating less, eating more, reducing fat/fibre/sugar
* waiting times for results from a blood test or biopsy
* remaining in hospital for observation

Look at the role play between a school nurse and a teenage boy who is being encouraged to change his diet (energy drinks, not eating breakfast, poor diet in general). Notice the way the nurse persuades Jake to make small changes in his diet to start with.

Setting: State School

Nurse: You are the school nurse at a state high school. You have been asked to speak to Jake Pullman, a 17 year old boy. He went to see a doctor one month ago and was told that he has scurvy (Vitamin C deficiency) but did not take it seriously or do anything about it. Now he has bruising and small haemorrhages on his legs. He has a poor diet and doesn't eat many foods which contain Vitamin C (citrus fruits e.g. oranges, mandarines etc)

Task:

1. Find out what Jake knows about scurvy – causes bruises and small blood spots, bleeding gums /loose teeth.

2. Explain scurvy and the causes (Vit C deficiency/lack of citrus in the diet) -

 ask questions about his diet.

3. Reassure Jake that his condition is treatable and reversible but only if he makes changes - dietary changes / may need vitamin C tablets.

4. Persuade Jake to make changes with his diet as it is important to avoid gum problems and tooth loss.

Setting: State school

Patient: You are Jake Pullman, a 17 year old boy who is attending a state high school. You are coming to see the nurse because you have bruises on your legs that are not going away. About a month ago you went to see a doctor and you were told that you had scurvy but you did not take it seriously. Now, you are a bit worried because the bruises are getting worse.

Task:

1. Explain that you've had bruises for a while and they are getting worse. The doctor said something about scurvy.

2. Explain that you are usually too rushed to have a proper breakfast. You just grab an energy drink on the way to school. You live with your Mum and she doesn't like cooking. You both eat a lot of fast food because it's easier.

3. Resist doing anything too difficult or that takes too much effort. How will you know what food you should eat? Can't you just have vitamin C tablets?

4. Finally understand that you need to do something. Agree to make small changes – you'll have orange juice instead of energy drinks.

Scurvy sample dialogue: watch the YouTube video at https://www.youtube.com/watch?v=1pcrcq0FOD0

Nurse: Hello Jake. Come on in.

Patient: (mumbling) Yeah right

Nurse: My name's Irene. I'm the school nurse here. I've been asked to talk to you about some problems you've been having in class lately.

Patient: (shrugs his shoulders) Mm

Nurse: Can you tell me a bit about what's going on at school at the moment?

Patient: I just get bored. I can't concentrate on what they're saying. I'm more worried about these bruises. And I've got all these red spots too.

Nurse: I see. Where's the bruising, Jake?

Patient: On my legs, all over them. And I've got these red spots everywhere.

Nurse: OK. Can I have a quick look?

Patient: (rolls up his trousers) There. Look.

Nurse: Oh yes. I can see why you're wondering about the bruises. Have you been to the doctor about the bruises?

Patient: Yeah, I went to the doctor a month ago. I went there and he said something about scurvy but that's only not having enough vitamin C. That won't cause these bruises.

Nurse: You wouldn't think so, would you? But it's right. Scurvy is a condition that you get if you are not getting enough Vitamin C in your diet. Vitamin C is important for making sure that your body can use iron properly. It also helps to strengthen the tissues of your blood vessels. If you don't have enough your gums will start bleeding and you'll bruise very easily.

Patient: Oh really? I didn't know that. The doctor just said I should eat better. Anyway , the drinks I drink have vitamins in them.

Nurse: Some drinks have added vitamin C but it's actually better to eat fresh fruit and vegetables. Do you eat a lot of fresh fruit and vegetables?

Patient: Um. No. I don't like fruit much. Mum doesn't like it either so she doesn't buy much.

Nurse: Can you tell me a bit more about your diet? What do you usually have for breakfast?

Patient: Well, um, I don't usually have time for breakfast. I just grab a red bull. It keeps me going. Sometimes I have two if I'm really tired.

Nurse: It is sometimes hard to find time for breakfast but energy drinks can be problem. They are full of caffeine. So if you have too many, you may get very restless. The drinks may be making it hard for you to concentrate in class.

Patient: I suppose. I dunno. I don't think about it.

Nurse: You said you don' fruit and vegetables?

Patient: Na. I don't like fruit and veges. Mum doesn't either so she doesn't buy any.

Nurse: I see. So you don't eat any fruit or vegetables and often skip breakfast and just have a red bull. Is that right?

Patient: Yeah. I don't have breakfast. I don't have time. I just grab a red bull on the way to school.

Nurse: OK, I understand. It does get busy in the mornings, I know. The thing is, Jake, that a vitamin C deficiency can be quite serious if it goes on too long. If you don't take in enough vitamin C your gums start bleeding and your teeth become loose. The worst case is that your teeth fall out. Don't worry, it's easy to fix but we need to talk about ways to do that.

Patient: I didn't know all that. I didn't think vitamins were that important.

Nurse: Yes, vitamins are important. Some vitamins can be stored in the body but vitamin C can't be stored for more than a short time. That's why I was asking whether you like fruit and vegetables. Vitamin C has to be taken in everyday because it isn't stored. The best source is in fruit and vegetables. Some have more vitamin C than others. I'm talking about citrus fruits like oranges and lemons and other fruit like kiwifruit, mangoes and strawberries. The best vegetables are cabbage, capsicum, spinach and broccoli.

Patient: So I can't just take a vitamin C pill?

Nurse: Well, you could take a tablet but it doesn't help you long-term. Do you like any of the fruit that I mentioned?

Patient: Um, I don't mind mangoes and kiwifruit are OK.

Nurse: That's great. Do you think you could make a mango smoothie for breakfast instead of having a red bull? They're quick to make and you could take it with you on the way to school.

Patient: Yeah, I suppose I could. I'd have to tell Mum to buy the fruit and stuff.

Nurse: Maybe your mother would like one too? I've got a brochure here about vitamin C and the food that is vitamin C rich. You could give that to your mother to read.

Patient: Yeah.OK.

Nurse: What about oranges? Do you like orange juice?

Patient: Yeah, it's OK.

Nurse: Maybe you could have an orange juice instead of a red bull at lunch-time.

Patient: Yeah, I could do that. So, you're saying that the bruises are because I don't have enough vitamin C?

Nurse: That's right. The bruises are a sign that you need more vitamin C, that you are not taking in enough vitamin C every day.

Patient: If I start getting more vitamin C, how long before the bruises go?

Nurse: If you start taking in vitamin C each day, the bruises will go quite quickly. As a teenage boy, you need around 75mg of vitamin C each day, more if you're a smoker. Remember that it can't be stored at all.

Patient: Yeah. I understand. I'll get onto it and get Mum to help as well. So, if I stop the red bulls, I'll be able to concentrate better?

Nurse: It should help a lot. Energy drinks have large amounts of caffeine in them. It makes you very restless speeds up your heart rate. Try to avoid them and see what difference it makes. Is there anything else you'd like to ask me, about what we've been talking about?

Patient: No, I don't think so.

Nurse: OK. If you need to ask any questions later, you know where my office is. Can you come and see me in a week to see how things are going?

Patient: Yeah, OK. I'll see you next week. Thanks for the information.

Nurse: That's OK. I'll see you next week, Jake.

10. Difficult conversations

People in distress can find it difficult to listen to what you are saying and may not be able to respond appropriately. One example of a difficult conversation is when dealing with aggressive patients or relatives.

Role plays which concern patients or relatives who are annoyed or angry can be challenging. There are some useful tools which can help you in dealing with these sorts of situations.

One of the main causes of frustration for patients and their relatives is delay in treatment, for example an operation which is postponed. It is important to try to imagine the emotions patients and relatives go through when this happens. Remember that the patient is probably anxious about the surgery and its outcome. They will have been fasting for several hours to prepare for the operation so they are probably hungry and thirsty.

Added to these emotions is the very powerful feeling of loss of control over their environment. Some unlucky patients have their operation postponed not just once but twice or three times. Sometimes an angry response results from the hope that it may influence the surgeon to go ahead with the operation anyway.

There are several actions which you should avoid when you are dealing with patients or relatives who are distressed or behaving in an aggressive manner. It is important not to try to restrain the person at all. This includes touching the person on the arm or shoulder and using restraints. Restraints can only be used after a medical assessment is made and a medical order is completed.

Try not to react to bad language – overlook language even if it is personal if possible. If the person is delusional, reorient them to reality. It is, however, important not to be defensive or blame someone else for the perceived problem. At all times attempt to calm the environment by asking the person to speak a little quieter so you can understand better.

A common cause of distress and anger in patients' relatives is delay in treatment. Look at the sample role play card for a nurse and imagine how you would react. Then, read the transcript of a dialogue between a nurse and the relatives of a patient whose operation has been delayed.

Sample role play:

Setting: Hospital Ward

Nurse: You have been called to the patient's bedside. The patient was supposed to go in for his surgery at 10 am (second on the list) but surgery was delayed because the patient (first on the list) had some complications during surgery. He had never had anesthesia before, was suffering from post op vomiting, hadn't passed urine and is in pain. The patient's daughter is very angry and wants to talk to you.

Task:

1. Find out why the patient's daughter is angry - use appropriate non-verbal communication.

2. Empathise with the daughter about the delay - be realistic.

3. Explain why the operation is late, try not to blame Operating Theatre staff but explain post op complications can be unavoidable.

4. Negotiate with the daughter to prevent her from insisting her father is discharged.

Transcript:

Nurse: Yes, Mr Bigley. You rang your buzzer. Can I help you?

Patient's daughter: No. It wasn't my father who called. It was me.

Nurse: Oh, OK. How can I help you?

Patient's daughter: Well, you can help by telling me why my father is still in his bed when he should be having his operation right now. I'm sick of this. You people are useless. How difficult is it to take an old man to his operation on time?

Nurse: I can see that you're very upset. Before we talk about it, I need to check with your father that it's OK with him for me to discuss this with you.

Patient's daughter: What do you mean? That just sounds like another delaying tactic to me!

Nurse: Yes. I know it must seem like that but it's important to make sure that your father gives permission for us to discuss his treatment. I'm sure you can understand that he has the right to agree or not to having his treatment discussed.

Patient's daughter: Oh.. well. I suppose I understand. Dad, you don't mind if I talk to the nurse about your operation, do you?

Patient: No, I don't mind if you talk to Sally about me.

Nurse: Thanks, Mr Bigley. It would help if I understood a bit more about the problem. Can you tell me a bit more about why you are upset?

Patient's daughter: Well, thank goodness. Finally someone is asking! I've been here with Dad for hours just sitting and waiting. He was supposed to go for his operation at 10 o'clock. He hasn't had a thing to eat or drink since yesterday. Someone just said he couldn't go for the operation yet but didn't tell us why. Now we don't have any idea when or if he'll have his operation. If it goes on too much longer, I'm going to take him home. It can't be worse than being here. I'm sick of the way you get treated here. No-one tells you anything.

Nurse: I can see why you must be very frustrated by all this. If I've understood you correctly, you are frustrated about the delay in the operation and feel that you haven't been kept informed of the reasons for the delay and when your father is likely to have his operation? Is that right?

Patient's daughter: Yes. That's about it. No-one has bothered to tell my father anything. They've just left him here starving and waiting for an operation that might never happen. It's not right doing that to an old man.

Nurse: It does seem very harsh when you haven't had a drink all night and are probably very hungry. I can help you out with that after we've had our chat, Mr Bigley. You can rinse your mouth out with a small amount of water as long as you don't swallow any.

Patient: That's sounds wonderful.

Patient's daughter: Well that's all very well and good but what about the rest of the problems?

Nurse: I know that the time for your operation was supposed to be 10 o'clock. I've just checked with Theatres to find out the reason for the delay. Apparently the patient who was first on the list, before your father, had a few difficulties after his operation. It has taken a bit of time to stabilise his vomiting.

Patient's daughter: That's not Dad's fault. Why should he have to wait?

Patient: Come on, Sally. These things happen.

Patient's daughter: No, Dad. These things don't just happen. They should know about these things and fix them.

Nurse: I can understand your feeling that way. Unfortunately, this was the first anaesthetic the patient has ever had before so no-one knew how he would react. The staff in Recovery think that he should be all right soon. That means that your father will be able to go for his operation.

Patient's daughter: Sounds like a cover-up. Dad, I think you should come home with me. I don't believe them at all.

Patient: Oh...I. I don't know, Sally.

Nurse: I know that it is hard when you have to wait so long but it is very important that you have your operation.

Patient's daughter: Well, I'm not so sure. If it was so important, you'd have made sure he had the operation on time.

Nurse: I agree that treatment schedules don't always go to plan but it really is very important that your father stays in hospital. Would you be willing to wait a bit longer before you make the decision to take your father home or not?

Patient's daughter: I don't know. Dad shouldn't wait around for ever.

Nurse: I understand what you are saying. If I keep you up to date with what's happening, would you be willing to wait a bit longer?

Patient's daughter: I guess so. As long as we know what's going on.

Nurse: Yes. I'll make sure that I tell you how long your father will be waiting.

Patient: Thank you, nurse. I would appreciate that.